Begging for It

Begging for It

Alex Dimitrov

Four Way Books
Tribeca

This book is for Rachel Silveri

I would walk through the fire for you

Please direct all inquiries to:
Editorial Office
Four Way Books
POB 535, Village Station
New York, NY 10014
www.fourwaybooks.com

Library of Congress Cataloging-in-Publication Data

Dimitrov, Alex.
  Begging for it : poems / by Alex Dimitrov.
    p. cm.
  ISBN 978-1-935536-26-0 (pbk. : alk. paper)
  I. Title.
  PS3604.I4648B44 2013
  811'.6--dc23

                        2012029323

This book is manufactured in the United States of America
and printed on acid-free paper.

Four Way Books is a not-for-profit literary press. We are grateful for the assistance
we receive from individual donors, public arts agencies, and private foundations.

This publication is made possible with public funds
from the National Endowment for the Arts

and from the New York State Council on the Arts, a state agency

 and from the Jerome Foundation.

[clmp] We are a proud member
of the Council of Literary Magazines and Presses.

Distributed by University Press of New England
One Court Street, Lebanon, NH 03766

Contents

I

II

III

IV

V

Notes

"What flag will I bear? What beast worship? What shrine besiege? What hearts break? What lies tell?—And walk through whose blood?"

—Arthur Rimbaud

I

Heartland

In America, I stopped to listen for God.
What about these men with their wolf tongues
and the war with its quick deaths and how vast
death is and how nothing fits in it.
Let the blood wet the ashes,
let the semen wet the mouth.
This man tonight is going inside
himself and let him stay there because
I could kill faster than any war would, God.

The Crucifix

It hung from his neck in a kind and devastating way—
hidden under his shirt and apron, wait-staff uniform
then blazer, when he finally found a good desk job.

Walking through the living room after work
he'd slowly loosen the knot of his tie, teasing it
with his fingers and unbuttoning that top button

every man must hate so much.
From there it took him only seconds
until the cotton trailed behind his back,

shirt fully undone, allowing me to notice
the tense drops of sweat which ran down from his armpits,
the stains forming delicate rings around his sleeves.

And when he sat down on the couch
to rest his head back, Adam's apple
sharply gleaming, palms left open on his thighs—

I'd stare at that gold crucifix which sank so low,
our Jesus buried deep inside his chest hair,
closer to my father than I ever got

and claiming the best part.

Passage

At the St. Mark's Baths Hart Crane washes my hair
and I tilt around the cold porcelain of the basin
with strain and delight, trying to look at him.

But before I meet his sea-tempered eyes
I feel his hands easing my head
into the dark water,

as if he were a sailor calming a storm
on a ship with insatiable men.
When he tugs at the ropes that are my hair

my American youth streams down—
one year so heavy, it finds its way under the towel
around my waist and rests near the curve of my thigh.

Who am I? I think. And I try to remember
the beginning of beauty—before Orpheus,
before winter—

before this man who sings
for the drowning, touches my lips,
and I ignite.

Leaving for America, May 1991

It didn't happen during the war, I remember that.
Because like everyone else we sat in front of the television and waited
for the American soldiers to leave the Gulf.

It was close to happening when my mother came home one day
and never went back to work.
She didn't tell anyone why.

Even closer when things in our apartment kept disappearing:
the vase on the table, old books, our small radio.
I found them in boxes one day.

Then it finally began at the airport
when our bags were too heavy to check
and we had to decide what to leave,

We can't keep everything, my father said.

And as the plane pulled away we tried sleeping
until mid-flight a stranger asked,
What time is it over there?

But none of us knew.

The ocean below warned
don't swim.

The country we'd left for
still felt at war.

And we didn't arrive even after the plane ride,
after the taxi, and in the new house

where for days we had nothing to say.

American Youth

That first summer my father spent more time
driving to work than he did sleeping,

and my mother wrote postcards all day
to everyone back home, people she never liked,

even they were needed, she said, to pass the time,
to live through the hours we had to fill with

English lessons—every day a new word, then phrases,
and finally sentences that spoke of nothing

no matter how many times they repeated in our ears.
I'd leave the house sometime after lunch

to sit on the sidewalk and imagine
that one of the cars driving by was my father's.

And every day there I watched the neighborhood
kids playing, watched them tirelessly until dark,

trading cards with each other, toy guns.
I watched them live out my American youth.

The Underwear

At seven I hadn't seen my father naked
but found the outline of what held him.
I stared at the loose waistband that snapped
around his hips, cupped the pouch
which was slightly darker, more worn
than the rest of the cotton.

Held high above my face, I pressed it down,
let it cover my eyes and nose, a kind of warm suffocation.
My knees gave in when I pulled at the cloth
with each tooth, bit into it.

The terror wasn't the pleasure—
more animal than another boy's hands
pressing my face into the playground dirt.
It was the moment she came in, looked
away, and like a good mother,
asked me to wash my hands before dinner.

Night Flights

One night before my father came
she caught me in the yard
counting off night flights, keeping tally.

The large machines sped over
loud and without grace.
Each one I pointed to the nearest airport.

And those which headed east
toward New York or some other city—
they made it.

The rest crashed suddenly in someone else's life.

St. Sebastian Questions a Terrorist

It's easy to forget Cain wandered for years
in a world without countries. In a desert
with no one to take him in—

a desert you found and began to study.
Tell me, what did you see there?
Were more people looking for God

than there were stories to tell?
And the soldiers, what did they look for?
When there was nothing to do

but question the darkness,
did your sorrow become the hostage
that wouldn't allow you to rest?

To the Thirsty I Will Give Water

Yesterday morning while I read Montaigne
a man drove his car into the Gowanus canal.

I have never seen a greater monster or miracle
than myself, Montaigne wrote in the late 16th century.

It was a bright day.
The sun forgave no one.

Not even the firefighter who first saw
the car taken by the water while he was praying,

lighting a cigarette, remembering his lover's face—
what was he doing, what did he think of before diving in?

It is not death, it is dying
that alarms me, Montaigne tells us.

Because he swallowed enough black water during the rescue
the firefighter was given two Hepatitis B shots afterward.

The man who lost his car was given his life back.
We were given Montaigne's heart

which is preserved in the parish church named after him
in the southwest of France.

We were given more than we can drown.

America, You Darling

After every needle finds its way inside me
I'm content and calm and easily turned on
by life. And then I'm here again, on Broadway,
wondering which direction promises
a cab, a God, a merciless mouth.
The world is not ending today
so it's important to stay in it.
It's the potential I'm in love with
when I sleep with someone new.
Like Washington will always love
the Washingtons around its sleazy waistband
(George, I too beg for you).
The slim go-go boy on Fridays
doesn't care about the past or future.
What turns him on?
Your bills (not marriage bills),
attention (not affection),
leaving early with a client, never
coming back. Is it him or Jesus
who lives here among us
and will die a modern death?
See, I don't like being heartless,
I'm not good at it, I quit.
I vote fast, depressed,
and every four years

though I'd like to see us happy,
quitting smoking, getting clean.
I stand in my underwear
before the flag, before another man
who promises a lot like our next President.
I have my filthy lips, my shiny teeth
and they are biting—I am biting
into a bloody overpriced steak
after years of being a vegetarian.

This Is a Personal Poem

My self's self is thinking about itself.
Trying to sell its self a new self.

Don't worry, reader,
I'm not trying to fool you with language,

I have eyes to do that with.
I have forgotten our history,

I have forgotten how we met.
Reader, are you upset at how fast we're moving?

I'm likely with you in your bed,
between your hands, somewhere

in your mouth before
whatever it is you'll say next.

Say *yes* and *now* and *love* too.
Say what did Judith Butler say when saying,

" . . . one is undone, in the face of the other,
by the touch, by the scent, by the feel,

by the prospect of the touch,
by the memory of the feel."

I want to know you, reader.
I want to know a lot of things.

Can we ever truly forget about ourselves?
Is every self a self that makes itself available to love?

Like death. And its kind availability.
Like language, reader,

would we still be so unhappy if we could escape it?
To name the namelessness that is love,

in what we read, and what we see,
and what are feelings really?

Facts or flaws,
or something tells me now

that I must leave you, reader.
It's not you, it's me.

We guess at why things end,
we ruin things, we start and stall,

and all all all we do
is want.

This Is Not a Personal Poem

This is not a personal poem.
I don't write about my life.
I don't have a life.
I don't have sex.
I have not experienced death.
Don't take this personally but
I don't have any feelings either.
The feelings I don't have don't run my life.
I have an imagination. I'm imagining it now.
This poem is concerned with language on a very plain level.
This poem stole that line from John Ashbery.
This poem wants you to like it,
please click "like."
This poem was written during a recession.
I'm so politically conscious
the word "politics" is in my poem.
This is not a New York poem.
There's not enough room for all the wars in this poem.
Gay marriage is now in this poem.
Have you liked this poem yet?
It was written in 2011 in New York and posted 11 minutes ago.
Would you sleep with the poet who wrote this poem?
Would you buy his book? Click here.
This poem loves language.
This poem has slept with other poems
written by poets who love language.
All poets love language.
Let's talk about language while people die.

This poem cares a lot but wants you
to think that it doesn't really care.
The speaker of this poem may have been
born in a former Communist country.
It may or may not matter.
I had an orgasm before writing this poem.
I have my sunglasses on while reading this poem.
Everyone is going to die
please don't take it personally.
The world. The world.
The world is blood-hot and personal.
I stole that line from Sylvia Plath.
Put your money on this poem.
I love the money shot.
This is not a personal poem.
This poem is only about Alex Dimitrov.

James Franco

I would sleep with James Franco as Allen Ginsberg
and Allen Ginsberg would sleep with James Franco
as James Dean. Woof, woof and a howl.
James Franco makes me growl.

At the office I think about James Franco
as more than just performance art.
At my desk and in my poems—
I take him seriously, I write into him real hard.

Woof, woof and a howl.
I even like to watch James Franco scowl.
Once at a New York loft party a famous poet said,
"You are your author photo."

James Franco, James Franco, I love you.

Prayer for the New Year

Already the businessman on Broadway forgives himself
for what will happen between him and the boy

who stops to ask for a cigarette,
his face illuminating like an icon's

above the clean strike of the match.
Tonight, love isn't enough for anyone out here.

Across the street the blond gives his body
to every man who believes—

and in this city of salt and worship,
there are few moments to touch him.

Saint or stranger, I still recklessly seek you.

II

Prayer in Hell's Kitchen

I need an image to begin
like the city needs another face

thrown to the pavement,
kneeled on and stained.

Hell's Kitchen knows
how to welcome a stranger.

Wilde ones, let us forgive
the bitter pill delivered

with each finger shoved down.
Forgive tasting Judas. Forgive nothing.

Here is the bed, dark like a true beginning.

We all enter the body alone
and only once.

We do not get to stay.

The Composer's Lover

We had an hour without music.
A nerve brightly turning in a closed room of the mind—

the heart's black pool, a word that expired into the air
and woke everything.

Your bed slid under an invisible knife.
What happened to us after meeting, when the right note claimed

Manhattan's May morning like an elegy
already moving through the living?

Today, we are among them. Here to unsettle each other,
to undress beside the piano—elegant and unmistakably his.

Once it has you, there is a mouth
that never releases. A faint circle in a field of rust

hanging on the wall. We are not there.
We are in our bodies.

Like teeth marks in a shirt you once saw falling off him.
The delicate taste of blood that passed between us

before lust, before anyone could forgive us.

Bloodletting

The gods have no choice
but to let us live a little—

they would die for comedy.
You and I today, we're like bad actors

in a black and white Fellini movie.
If you can't show red, why bother filming?

The scene where the boys undress
and color the river with sex

is useless, like bloodletting.
And the pistons of the heart, the heart—

aren't pumping fast enough
to let us feel this thrashing.

Self-Portrait as Brigitte Bardot in *Contempt*

In the theater of bitters
where we sharpen,

I am your favorite actress.

The curtains sway, safe in their red light;
the props, once used, still gleam—

because even our own end loves us.

And here, stage left
I bow over you and listen

to the hot, uneven rhythm of your pulse.

It tells me you are deserving—
you accept this gift, this black collar

I tighten around your neck, this final kindness.

In the Museum of Old Lovers

The city we met in was never painted
as a *Still Life with an Open Drawer* to small happiness.

If I move through this life without stillness—
if I run my fingers over the paint

and what Cézanne has left out.

In bed, a man once asked
to be blindfolded while another choked me.

But in the end our ghosts find us three ways.
Through the familiar fist a body will bleed for—

heaving under the sheets—
and by every mouth we open for in the dark.

The third way refuses metaphor.

Although, I will tell you
how I still hear the waves breaking—

a ruined night music over your face.

Lush

I couldn't tell if it was you
or the man in the painting

standing beside me—
but I followed someone

down the narrow corridor
which opened to a room:

a gold field—emotional
in luster, like waves are.

And somewhere between feeling,
we disappeared

into that brightness—
and needed no word

to tell of our grief.

At Close Range

A burst of birds shooting up the morning—

a slow parting. A hiss.
A stranger's mouth that once pinned

its brief message—unread letters
spilled on the bed.

And the plane overhead takes no one away.

It's not easy to rise.
To live once.

Why do the teeth survive the body?

Seduce, rip open,
they season the flesh.

While the day singes your shirt,
knowing you have yet to meet him.

Don't worry. No one is spared.

In This Economy Even Businessmen Go Down

A man, like the market, can surprise you—

study him carefully while he uses your face
as a mirror, a screen.

When he unbuttons his shirt
he is teaching you kindness

and ruin he learned from his father—

leaving a wife and two kids, the crash at the office,
for a boy with your kind of eyes.

Suit & Tie, 6'1, Married, Financial District

Although I please when taken like a pistol,
cool in the mouth and without aftertaste—

he kindly asks to have me by the neck.
How much, and would you like to

come with me to Rome?
Or by the water somewhere?

Outside the Vatican—
who wouldn't drown there?

Yes, the saints are all I need to steer me.
This scent of him held one breath longer—

a check—another zero—and I'm yours.

Minor Miracles

Like a girl gone missing in her lone white dress,
I walk the bridges of this city

looking for someone to taste the sea with.
I grow still and the birds grow still with me.

I let my hair wrap around my neck.

Gentle boy, remove the knife—
but sweetly, sweetly.

Burn the bed
in which I no longer wait for you.

Begging for It

He crosses the dead avenue,
walks toward you, and loosens his ring

the way you imagine your father once did
on some night he still hasn't returned from.

Men you've lived with
and men you live on.

Whose scent will your knuckles keep?

His jaw clenches because your blood mixes sweetly
with the flower under his tongue,

the marquee's cheap glint,
each cab that passes and won't stop.

It's the night before Easter.
You do not forget it.

How the body becomes a cage you can't feel your way out of—

how God rips through the skin
of every man you know,

on a quiet evening,
in a city already done for, like this one.

All Souls' Day

Before I leave here, I want
to hear my name change in the mouth

of another animal.
Let it take long.

He'll want what I wanted from you—
blood at its richest,

most luminous, in that first moment
it touches the air.

Like the hunted
I need the day's sharpness—

deeper water,
something alive to sift

through me and kill.

Seven Chambers of a Wolf's Heart

And then I asked to kneel down with the pack—
to quiet the death choir
which hissed through my teeth.

My mouth—I let him lash it.

And watched while his panic slowly became us.

The seventh time I threw myself at him
something else took me.

III

Beginning in Buenos Aires

Our saints, unlike us, live on offerings of fire.

I knelt and lit three candles,
lost in the streets of Borges.

Who will sit with you in the burning room?
Who will admit you?

There was no one to count the hours with at La Recoleta—

city of the dead, of mausoleums with marble staircases
for those who will rise one day.

Among roses and rosaries
the mind forgets itself.

My life, with each candle, sparked on the altar—

spilled over gently.
I let the wax burn my knees

but I knew how to stand in the empty church.
Without God or pity.

A Second Heart Swims Up My Throat

The man in bed offers me three things.
We are led to a field

where my church ties are hung on the necks
of slim boys. They part my hair.

Tonight, I am the star of a surgery
where each organ is weighed in their hands.

Do you know you carry a soldier's piano inside you?
And with his tongue, the man

closes my eyelids for hours.
There is a rib I can never adjust in me,

a second heart swims up my throat.
When they pull the sheet over our bodies I hear Baudelaire say:

cruelty and sensual pleasure are identical.
I try to touch them like I would a blade coming toward me—

in the final scene each nerve is pounded close up.

Self-Portrait as Daisy in *The Great Gatsby*

When I walk in he is playing Chopin—
balcony doors open, drinks thinning in ice.

Outside an ambulance carries someone.

I sit in the chair next to the piano
to study how his face changes before the coda.

Why does it feel easier to live during a sonata?

In our letters, there are too many
hard vowels between us—

I always watch for the longest day of the year and then miss it.

It is early in the century and all the men are late.
I wait for everyone to leave the party.

For the music to end.

                    To feel the last note.

Sensualism

While lying in bed I think about sensualism.
A mosquito presses into my skin
with such cruelty I mistake it for love.

The stranger above my window decides to jump
and doesn't. Where was I?
I was opening the door to your life

and mine. We have some words
for each other and then what?
We have some nights in a city

next to an ocean filled with
more longing than we can describe.
I want to place your hand close to the knife

and let it sit there. I want more
than the cut or how we'll gently spill out.
The mosquito will drink

for as long as I'll let it. And I do.
I hold still waiting for you. The vein rises.
It is this flood of living that comes.

The Burning Place

These godless hours remain
the mind's faithful partner.
And from the only body I'll have,

I watch you motion, I watch you let me in.

Sontag recognized love is about submission.
Like giving yourself to be flayed and knowing
that any moment the other person can walk off

with your skin, she wrote.
If red is what I wear to dinner with you
to protect the skin I should give up.

If I say what you refuse to feel

and gladly take you to the burning place.
Where there is no you or I
and our veins, like graves, are opening

for what will open in us.
We start and finish one another with a kiss,
a look. We do it ruthlessly and all the time.

After Love

In the first poem I wrote after you left, I killed you.
My hand met the back of your neck
and lead you to water, where I held your hair—
under—one last time.

But this is the poem I've kept—
it's years ago and we're in bed.
Night slips into morning and I realize
I've woken up early again to watch you dress,

to remember you,
even though you're right there, next to me.

A Lover's Discourse

Last night, Roland Barthes reminded me
I am a prisoner condemned to death

before he is led to the scaffold.
Last night, because the apartment was beautifully empty

I set out on the bed, with great attention,
the clothes I last wore

when we were together—
a simple black shirt, faded gray denim

and the jacket you said had a heart pocket.
I hovered above them for a long time

noticing where your tongue used to press itself
to the stitching, where the threads frayed

exposing something about their origin.
I laid down and draped the black

over my neck so we touched
like always—so carelessly.

I got up slowly, putting each garment on.
I did this for the entire night.

His Red Ribs, Glittering

Now that it's over, let it move
through me like water.

Outside the birds keep flight
toward each the other,

a boy falls and his blood
brightens the snow.

The year begins and I can't tell
how the days hold together,

can't tell your hair—on the bed,
in my mouth—from my own.

Uncomplicated Happiness

Maybe I don't want uncomplicated happiness.
In the morning one of us turns
to dress away from the other
although little has changed.
In a better world memory would
always lead back to affection.
Who is that person on the edge
of the bed, looking back?
Nothing is uncomplicated, traveler.
Maybe I wanted you to stay
for the wrong reasons.
Maybe it's the wrong reasons I love.
I too am somewhere over an ocean—
writing you this as fast as I can.

Grave Flowers

With Brahms and my bag, I left
the city's bright satellites—connect
here, remember nothing, repeat.

Far from you in every way
people know to measure distance,
in this house where solitude fits,

you are the first person I think of
walking through the empty rooms
and into my study, where we are

what I study. I am learning to live
without the city. I think red thoughts
built softly, like music.

Because this place holds nothing of us,
the neighbor's bird came to die
by the front door.

It did not want to be rescued. It fought
against touch. Every morning
the light surprises me.

I allow a moment for the feeling
to reach seduction, to reach in. Yesterday
the small body was gone.

No mark where it last suffered—
touch, air, the sound of a late car
breaking our human barrier.

I would like no one to visit me here,
but I thought to write you and say
there are seven trees on the path

to the field with grave flowers.
I imagine we walked to the sixth
and turned back.

Without words is how
we are taken. Without words
the night offers her hand.

The Fates

They gather in a white room arranging flowers and singing.
I stand beside each woman as she makes choices—
a hyacinth added and shifted toward

lilac, a few nightshades around the edge
of the vase, and always two flowers taken away
for each new one added.

If this was a painting and not a dream,
I'd study its surface a long time and wonder
where the light comes from.

The frame sparks as a door
opens and the image begins
to dissolve—

only the hands of the women are visible.
I can't follow their movements or distinguish
the color of the blossoms whose stems

sink in vases filled with more light
than water, more light than matter,
shadow, or flesh.

Be careful, one sings to another
and the unmistakable pitch of glass breaking
again and again,

three times I hear it—three vases.
I'm not sure if I've stopped listening
or if the room is silent.

The canvas disappears, the dream recedes,
and somewhere my future takes a long pause,
then continues—

Fugue in the Wrong Key

Your face under the red sheets—
the city in fog.

Who has bought flowers for the lonely girl on the corner?
She carries them like the last thing she has.

I would like to stop and look at
more than a tragedy.

I would like to tell our story in rain.

In postmodern times, they read books with vanished characters
but took difficult lovers.

On the day I woke up there was no news of terror,
nothing to plan.

It was like the dead wake—to the softest sound.

Evening

This city you live in, terrified, is now empty.
Friends fly in and out—for love,

sometimes for nothing. And this evening,
a mist so fine your lips are slick

as you walk from his apartment to his
and then back, into yourself.

There is a place everyone leaves for.

Someone you slept with once said that to you
while he ran his hands over your face.

And there is a place for those still here,
watching the last ships circle around the receding island.

Blue Curtains

That day we were in a room with blue curtains.
Every time I wanted to speak
some hand would lift that pale, translucent fabric
and I'd see him standing on the circular balcony
which held something old and shapeless.
It was late morning.
We were already late for everything.
So I stood at one end of the room
and watched him. And between us
was a bed and a table and things
in a hotel—you know,
things that are anonymous
and belong to no one.
Like a sea or a life.
And all I remember is how expensive it was.
Not the room, but the feeling.

White Fire

To describe how rain touches morning in Iceland—
where St. Christopher often leads travelers
in spring—is to cross the impossible
bridge between water to drink
and water that drowns.

If you're lonely enough, if you listen,
the wind will convince you, in its human-like
sadness, to open the windows
and let something in.

Watch as it lifts above the ice—
the unforgiving element—white
fire.

Remember, you too know something
about snow's passage to water:

how everything trembles when moving
from one form to another—how soon,
it is water that slicks your eye—
each lash burning
to put the fire out.

IV

Self-Portrait Without the Self

On the edges of the body is where I stood,
trying to feel my way to the center.

For years, it was all I wanted.
Clawing at the small cells,

kicking in the bones to make room
for something more permanent.

And this morning, tired of my lips,
the way my hair will sometimes tilt

to one side, a lover of extremes,
every part of me, slanted

as if toward another body—
I no longer want the center:

this heart, or what's in it.
I want what isn't mine

and what will not last.
And yes, your heart will not last.

21st Century Lover

It's a miracle we keep living.

The sex we want most will kill us,
another war glitters on the horizon—

(forgive us)—obsession
no longer turns into pleasure,

though we yield to each terror
and ask to be taken gently.

Oscar Wilde once wrote that,
When the gods wish to punish us,

they answer our prayers.
I pray to be lifted yet remain here.

What do you pray for?
What part of you is worth saving?

What part of me can I give you to sell?

I Will Be Loving

Someone on the internet tells me,
"If we ever meet, I will lovingly degrade you."
Someone I don't know but want to.
I don't know my own father.
Not the way he wanted to be known,
not even the way I wanted him.
Every time I have sex I am leaving the town
I was born in again and for good.
Every time I walk into a bedroom
I pretend to be someone I'm not
interested in talking about in poems.
The first man who kissed me
also put his entire fist in my mouth.
The last man inside me
wouldn't even kiss me.
I am always inside me.
I am always inside.
I will lovingly degrade myself.
I will lovingly degrade myself for you.
I will degrade myself, reader.
For you.
I will be loving.

I'm Lonely and I Love It

I could call up Michael who I slept with recently
or James before him. I could go to another
this or that downtown and act a mess
in my best jeans. I could pretend
something really terrible happened
and cry, and make everyone bum me one cigarette
after another. I'm in Paris,
sorry I can't talk right now.
That's a great lie, a great line.
When really, here I am boys!
On my bed and in my underwear
doing absolutely nothing.
Playing with my hair,
playing sad ridiculous pop songs.
Let's face it, I'm lonely.
I'm lonely and I love it.

Sleeping with Everyone

In New York no one will do you a favor
unless you sleep with them
and then you may have to sleep with them
again. And again after that.

I wonder if I should start doing pornography
for more money. I wonder if I could role-play
as a plumber or a psychotic
youngish writer who wears leather

and takes it real hard in a walk-up on Allen St.
But wait, that's me! I should stop writing
personal poems. This is getting ridiculous.
O, it's another bloody day and everything screams

until he says, "My therapist thinks you're like cigarettes,"
before he says, "You're charming but so crazy."
After everyone I know has died a little and come back
and look! I'm off buying another life I can't afford because

I'm single, taken and in love.

Heroines

Just now a wave bleaches the sand white
in my book, a taxi veers off Fifth
where I walk reading, street water all over
a woman's skirt, the heroine lucky to be
alive and on shore, no man
on the next page.

Fast, isn't it?
Some mist and then some more.
A man, a car, good heroines know
both stall.

Woman with the drowned skirt—
don't go home.

I have written an entire day for you.

Self-Portrait as Brett in *The Sun Also Rises*

The last time I saw him he wore another life
with the tie I gave him in spring.

In the space between his cufflink and wine glass
I tried to collect myself—

was it Paris, or perfume on my wrists?

You don't want to mix emotions with wine, he said.
You lose the taste.

All day I have circled the same cafés.
Women like to sing a red song no matter who's listening.

Life could be darling, I thought during my cigarette.

We could live on devotional glances—
and take dinner in our best black, on the Champs-Élysées.

Radiance

I keep a note
a friend left in a book of photos:

lavender light over the snow flats—

and I wonder if he used it in a poem,
or if seeing, if the pleasure, was enough?

Now that you and I aren't lovers

I notice how the light at times
will race up your obedient body,

and reveal the flame I looked for—

the life I said I saw,
and hoped would be enough.

Red Desert

I think of you the way I do of the pyramids.
Because there were men who slaved for their beauty,
does it cost more to love them?

One ordinary Monday I left my life
and took a plane without telling anyone—
to that place where the digging happens.

I wanted to lift the stones
and weigh them in my hands.
I wanted to throw something back.

You see, there is disagreement among scholars
about the methods Egyptians used to move
the limestone and granite they built with.

Maybe you've seen the photographs—
inside the tombs of the Twelfth Dynasty.
Scenes of daily life on the walls:

170 men pulling a sixty ton statue,
dragging it with a wooden sledge and ropes.
How much faith in something

fuels that kind of pulling?
Or like us, is it ritual, obedience,
and punishment that arrest them?

When this life becomes nothing
but the hauling of stone,
a burden begun on a night years ago,

the pyramids may look to us
a slow deep red at sundown. To see them,
we face the desert without choice.

Nowhere Better Than This Place

Descending over the billboards and all they promise—
it's easy to forget we're alive in all this.

Some days I try to feel without language:

like the sky tells us everything
by the palette it shares with grief.

You die faster if you can't find a metaphor

is what I see in the eyes of the Virgin.
So I leave some of myself in that last wind

before landing, when the plane can be taken
anywhere, nowhere—

somewhere better than this place.

Refusing the Ledge

For months only travelers and the dead
touching you. In hotel rooms higher

than a summer suicide—laced with sugars
and sweat, the steps from the interior

to the ledge. An address book, a book of names,
someone's life laid open in bed.

So when he spoke to you
your hair grew a shade darker

and his voice felt cooler
than the pavement outside—

where a child lost his only possession,
a balloon deflating through his ribs.

How brief, how brilliant
the minutes felt in their unkindness.

And you chose to be touched
instead of touching down.

We Are a Natural Wonder

Suppose I never make it to San Francisco
or stop trying to describe the light in Paris

in those brief violet hours between three and five
when we are permitted happiness.

Suppose that's not true at all.
How there may be nothing to say about light

or the way emotion seizes the body
imprecisely, indefinitely.

We are the animals who can't leave things at wonder.
We want wonderful, we would kill for it.

Somewhere in New York I take the moon into my mouth,
under my tongue, over the black earth.

I'm looking for one secret about people
no matter the season or city or how dark their eyes are.

Arrivals, departures, few words, less wonder.
If it's rain we are least like, let us be rain.

The Why

I want to be in rooms full of people I love.
The world goes white then green again
like the mind telling the body it is not alone.
The body saying something I can almost hear
above the sound of a dog barking
because he feels himself tied and tremendously alone.
Who would you believe?
I walk the great streets of New York City
where many great people have lived
and think how great it is to live and die on earth
even if it means having known nothing
of the why. Nothing of the why.

Dear Friend: I have nearly died three times since morning

For a long time I would not go to bed.

You'll remember those months and the sky
like the tip of a finger dipped in wax.

Every time I felt pleasure I held my breath—

why did you write over that line in your letter?
The snow made me forget how hot the blood is.

How another person can step into a room
as if out of a painting,

and offer me a life.

Can you feel which part of your body this poem goes to?
Your fingers or teeth,

the top of your chest—
does it touch your face?

I was thinking we could see each other again.

At night, with our masks on,
so we know exactly who to look for.

I'll read you this fragment of Proust

before the next snowfall, so neither us of will forget . . .
the better part of our memory exists outside us,

in a blatter of rain, in the smell of an unaired room . . .

Darling

The days fall out of your pockets one after the other.
Soon you'll need a new jacket with tougher leather

and seams no one has felt. Soon you'll bring
the old books into your bed and sleep easy

and alone. It must be December again.
This must be the part of the story where you

refuse to say how the bodies you've walked toward
continue walking in you. With heavy black boots

in a calm procession of *darling* and *honey*—
they walk up and down the narrow streets of your heart.

v

I'm Always Thinking About You, America

A way for us to begin when beginnings have passed us.
Before you saw him you knew exactly where you wanted to put your hands.
Casually, the light in that room became what you remembered of summer.
Days of slow mornings, days of nothing but nights.
Even in a time like ours, war ends and love too.
For now I will write about love.
Going every day to that place in you that is homeless.
How quiet you were the first time you saw your mother cry.
I'm always here, yes, writing or thinking about you.
Just like that it was autumn and not spring for a long time.
Kindness was somewhere in his hands, how they shook after crossing the border.
Listening to Glass and then Brahms to feel changed, suddenly.
Mundane pleasures: coffee, orgasm, a walk down First Street.
Nights that return in the daytime and you need to sit down.
Oh I want to stop here, what more can I tell you?
President Clinton on television while we were children.
Quietly typing in a square of light in a room where you lived while people died.
Reason is not needed with us, he said.
So, "I want to know who you are," who the "I," who the "we" is.
Today I am returning to everyone at least once in my mind.
Until I die I want to keep telling Rachel I love her.
Voices in the house where you grew up in an afternoon, in one gaze.
What do we look for when we say, "Where are you going right now?"
Xoxoxoxo   x
Years that pass fast and slowly through us.
Zero apologies today but of course, there were things we did and didn't do.

Notes

"Leaving for America, May 1991" is for my mother and father

"This Is Not a Personal Poem" is for CA Conrad

"Lush" is inspired by Roni Horn's *Gold Field*, 1980-82

"Self-Portrait as Daisy in *The Great Gatsby*" borrows the italicized line in the poem from F. Scott Fitzgerald's *The Great Gatsby*

"White Fire" is for Anne Carson

"Heroines" is for Dorothea Lasky

"Self-Portrait as Brett in *The Sun Also Rises*" borrows the italicized lines in the poem from Ernest Hemingway's *The Sun Also Rises*

"Nowhere Better Than This Place" is inspired by Felix Gonzalez-Torres's *Somewhere Better Than This Place/Nowhere Better Than This Place*, 1990

"The Why" is for Marie Howe

"Dear Friend: I have nearly died three times since morning" takes its title from a letter by Marcel Proust

Acknowledgments

Thank you to the editors of the following journals, magazines and anthologies where these poems first appeared:

Alaska Quarterly Review, American Poetry Review, Anti–, The Awl, Bellevue Literary Review, Best New Poets 2009, Boston Review, Boxcar Poetry Review, The Cortland Review, Crab Orchard Review, Gay & Lesbian Review, From the Fishouse, Harpur Palate, H.O.W., I Am a Natural Wonder, The Journal, Kenyon Review, Lambda Literary, LA Review, Linebreak, The Literary Review, New York Quarterly, The Paris-American, Poet Lore, Poor Claudia, Portland Review, RevolutionESQUE, Salmagundi, Slate, Southwest Review, Tablet, Tin House, Underwater New York, Women's Studies Quarterly, and *The Yale Review.*

"Passage" was featured on Poetry Daily on July 26, 2011.

"White Fire" also appeared as a broadside in a limited edition of 100 as part of the Broadsides Reading Series at the Center for Book Arts in New York City.

"Darling" was the recipient of the 2011 Stanley Kunitz Prize from the *American Poetry Review.*

So many people have helped me—whether talking with me about the poems in this book or about the greater force that is poetry.

I'm forever grateful to my mother and father, Mark Bibbins, Frank Bidart, Laure-Anne Bosselaar, Traci Brimhall, Gabrielle Calvocoressi, Anne Carson, CA Conrad, Michael Cunningham, Timothy Donnelly, Mark Doty, Jorie Graham, Linda Gregg, Deborah Landau, Ada Limón, Thomas Lux, Randall Mann, David McConnell, Raymond McDaniel, J. D. McClatchy, Honor Moore, Thylias Moss, Angelo Nikolopoulos, Robert Pinsky, Victoria Redel, Martha Rhodes, Tree Swenson, Keith Taylor, Mark Wunderlich, and everyone at the Academy of American Poets and Four Way Books.

Thank you to St. Mary's College of Maryland for having me as their writer-in-residence in April and May of 2010, and to Karen Anderson and Jerry Gabriel, for the beautiful time I spent at St. Mary's, writing poems that found their way here.

Alex Bacon, you read and were there for the first poems in this book. They remind me of you and I love that.

Tom Healy, everything changed when I met you. Thank you for helping me with my poems, for your generosity, and for being a real gentleman.

Brenda Shaughnessy, thank you for being my friend, for your poems, and for teaching me by example.

Dorothea Lasky, your love and support are endless and I'll be thanking you endlessly. I'm lucky to have you as a friend.

Marie Howe, you are the light in these poems and my poetry mother. I'm so happy to be living in this world with you. I remember the first time I met you and you believed in me even when I didn't. Thank you.

Rachel Silveri, you make everything possible. This book has always been for you. I love you.

Oscar Wilde, you are my patron saint. I will not disappoint you.

Alex Dimitrov is the recipient of the Stanley Kunitz Prize from the *American Poetry Review* and the founder of Wilde Boys, a queer poetry salon in New York City. His poems have been published in *American Poetry Review, Boston Review, Kenyon Review, Poetry Daily, Slate, Tin House, The Yale Review,* and he is the author of *American Boys*, an e-chapbook published by Floating Wolf Quarterly. He is a program coordinator at the Academy of American Poets, teaches creative writing at Rutgers University, and frequently writes for *Poets & Writers* magazine.